L·O·S·T F·O·R·E·V·E·R

EXTINCT
ANIMALS OF THE
ISLANDS

Barbara J. Behm and Jean-Christophe Balouet

Gareth Stevens Publishing
MILWAUKEE

For a free color catalog describing Gareth Stevens' list of high-quality books and multimedia programs, call 1-800-542-2595 (USA) or 1-800-461-9120 (Canada).
Gareth Stevens Publishing's Fax: (414) 225-0377.
See our catalog, too, on the World Wide Web: http://gsinc.com

The editor would like to extend special thanks to Jan W. Rafert, Curator of Primates and Small Mammals, Milwaukee County Zoo, Milwaukee, Wisconsin, for his kind and professional help with the information in this book.

Library of Congress Cataloging-in-Publication Data available upon request from publisher. Fax (414) 225-0377 for the attention of the Publishing Records Department.

ISBN 0-8368-1525-4

This North American edition first published in 1997 by
Gareth Stevens Publishing
1555 North RiverCenter Drive, Suite 201
Milwaukee, Wisconsin 53212 USA

Picture Credits
Eric Alibert: title, pp. 5, 8, 10, 12, 13, 14, 18, 19, 24, 25, 26, 27; British Museum of Natural History: pp. 20 (bottom), 21; National Library: Cover, pp. 6, 7, 17, 22, 23

Series editor: Patricia Lantier-Sampon
Series designer: Karen Knutson
Additional picture research: Diane Laska
Map art: Donna Genzmer Schenström, University of Wisconsin-Milwaukee Cartographic
     Services Laboratory
Series logo artwork: Tom Redman

Printed in the United States of America

1 2 3 4 5 6 7 8 9 01 00 99 98 97

INTRODUCTION

For millions of years, during the course of evolution, hundreds of plant and animal species have appeared on Earth, multiplied, and then, for a variety of reasons, vanished. We all know of animals today — such as the elephant and the rhinoceros, the mountain gorilla and the orangutan — that face extinction because of irresponsible human activity or changes in environmental conditions. Amazingly, hundreds of species of insects and plants become extinct before we can even classify them. Fortunately, in modern times, we are beginning to understand that all living things are connected. When we destroy a plant species, we may be depriving the world of an amazing cure for human diseases. And we know that if we destroy the forest, the desert creeps forward and the climate changes, wild animals die off because they cannot survive the harsh conditions, and humans, too, face starvation and death. Let us remember that every creature and plant is part of a web of life, each perfect, each contributing to the whole. It is up to each of us to end the destruction of our natural world before it becomes too late. Future generations will find it hard to forgive us if we fail to act. No matter what our age or where we live, it is time for every one of us to get involved.

Dr. Jane Goodall, Ethologist

CONTENTS

Words that appear in the glossary are printed in **boldface** type the first time they occur in the text.

ISLANDS

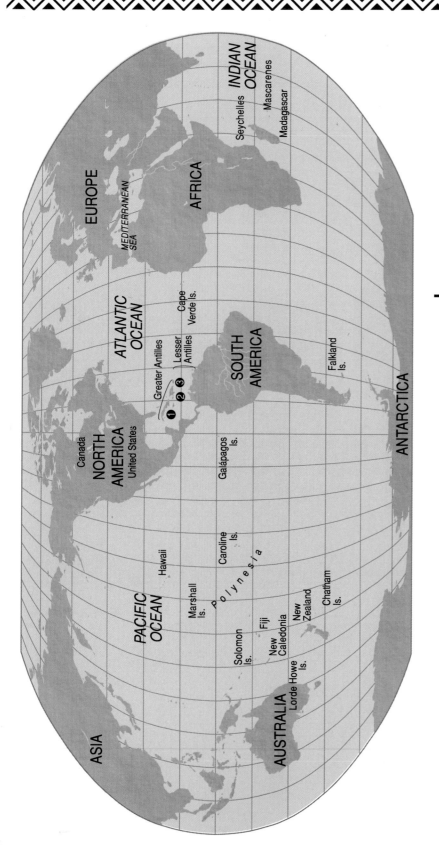

The map shows the continents and oceans of the world with the following labeled:

Oceans and Seas: PACIFIC OCEAN, ATLANTIC OCEAN, INDIAN OCEAN, MEDITERRANEAN SEA

Continents: ASIA, EUROPE, AFRICA, NORTH AMERICA, SOUTH AMERICA, AUSTRALIA, ANTARCTICA

Islands and places: Canada, United States, Hawaii, Marshall Is., Caroline Is., Solomon Is., Fiji, New Caledonia, New Zealand, Chatham Is., Lorde Howe Is., Polynesia, Galápagos Is., Greater Antilles, Lesser Antilles, Cape Verde Is., Falkland Is., Seychelles, Mascarenes, Madagascar

MAP KEY:
- ❶ Cuba
- ❷ Hispaniola (Haiti and Dominican Republic)
- ❸ Puerto Rico

▲ Many species of plant and animal life on Earth have become extinct, and many more are in imminent danger. This tragic situation is not limited to any one place; it is a global problem. From the northern and southern continents to the islands of Earth's oceans and seas, numerous animal species have disappeared forever. Only the intervention of human resources may now be able to save currently endangered animals. This map indicates some of the continents, countries, bodies of water, and other areas referred to in *Lost Forever: Extinct Animals of the Islands.*

VANISHED SPECIES

Countless animal species in Earth's oceans and seas have been lost forever. The 41 million square miles (105 million sq. kilometers) of the Atlantic Ocean are home to only a few hundred islands. The West Indies, also called the Antilles, forms the biggest **archipelago** in the Atlantic. These islands are the most densely populated islands of the world. This overpopulation has resulted in forest destruction and the **extinction** of more than forty **species** of birds and mammals. Several human groups were also exterminated by the Europeans. Half a million Arawak Indians of the Antilles were entirely killed off.

The Caribbean monk seal, *Monachus tropicalis*, has been hunted into extinction by humans. The seal's fur and meat brought about a rapid extinction in the mid-twentieth century.

▲ The Caribbean monk seal, *Monachus tropicalis*, became extinct in about 1954, the only species of seal destroyed by humans so far.

The great auk, *Pinguinis impennis*, was hunted by the tens of millions for its meat, feathers, and fat. It was extinct by 1844.

THE WEST INDIES

As with most tropical islands, a rich **fauna**, particularly of birds, had developed here. The main causes for extinctions of many species were overhunting by humans and the introduction of predatory mammals, such as the rat and mongoose.

BIRDS

Siphonornis americanus was a nightjar native to Jamaica. The last pair was captured in 1850. This species became extinct due to hunting by humans and **introduced predators**, especially cats.

A group of birds that has suffered great losses due to humans is the parrots. Some of the parrot species that have

▲ The great auk, *Pinguinis impennis*, was hunted by the tens of millions by humans and became extinct by 1844.

perished as a result of overhunting by humans include the Cuban macaw, *Ara tricolor*; the Jamaican yellow-headed macaw, *Ara gossei;* the orange-bellied macaw of Martinique, *Anodorhynchus martinicus*; and the violet macaw of Guadeloupe, *Anodorhynchus purpurescens*.

▲ The Jamaican yellow-headed macaw, *Ara gossei*, was extinct by 1765.

MAMMALS

The Martinique giant rice rat, or pilori, *Megalomys demarestii*, was overhunted by humans. The last of these muskrats sought refuge on the slopes of Mt. Pelée. However, the eruption of Mt. Pelée in 1902 killed the few remaining members of this species.

Isolobodons (hutia) of the Dominican Republic and Puerto Rico were hunted for their meat. The Haitian species, *Isolobodon levir*, and the Puerto Rican species, *Isolobodon portoricensis*, are both extinct.

Some large **edentate**, or toothless, mammals, such

▲ The Falklands fox, *Dusicyon australis*, disappeared in 1876.

as the Cuban ground sloth, *Megalocnus*, survived for only a while after the arrival of human settlers.

Two species of rice rats, *Oryzomys antillarium* of Jamaica and *Oryzomys victus* of St. Vincent Island, disappeared in 1877 and 1897, respectively. Their extinctions were probably brought about by introduced mongooses.

FALKLAND ISLANDS

The Falklands fox, *Dusicyon australis*, became extinct by 1876 mainly because of the thriving fur trade. It was also destroyed because some people accused the animal of vampirism.

The king penguin, *Aptenodytes*, disappeared from the Falklands due to the fur trade and the use of the penguins' oil to caulk ships and houses.

▲ The extinct St. Helena hoopoe is known only from fossil bones.

SAINT HELENA, CAPE VERDE, TRISTAN DA CUNHA

Introduced goats and other animals have caused great destruction to many native animals of Saint Helena. The giant skink, *Macroscincus coctaei*, of the Cape Verde Islands was hunted into extinction in the 1940s by humans. On Tristan da Cunha, in the South Atlantic, a native moorhen, the Tristan gallinule, *Gallinula nesiotis*, was destroyed by hunting and introduced rodent and canine predators before 1900.

PACIFIC OCEAN

EARTH'S LARGEST OCEAN

The Pacific Ocean is Earth's largest body of water. It occupies one-third of the planet's surface and contains about 25,000 islands, more than the total in the rest of the oceans combined. Few native animals, except for bats, have survived on the Pacific islands.

Research continues to uncover the existence of species whose disappearance was brought about by the first human inhabitants of the Pacific islands. Birds were the primary target. These bird species were hunted by humans for their feathers and flesh. The birds were also hunted by introduced predators, such as dogs and pigs that came with European settlers in the eighteenth century. Reptiles, and particularly lizards, also suffered greatly from hunting by humans.

BERING ISLAND

The gigantic Steller's sea cow, *Hydrodamalis stelleri*, belonged to the Sirenia family, a group of large, aquatic, plant-eating mammals. Steller's sea cow became extinct by 1768. The Bering Island spectacled cormorant, *Phalacrocorax perspicillatus*, was extinct by 1850. The cormorant

▲ The Bering Island spectacled cormorant, *Phalacrocorax perspicillatus*, was hunted by humans for food.

▲ Steller's sea cow, *Hydrodamalis stelleri*, was even larger than the manatees and the dugongs that are now the only survivors of the Sirenia family.

weighed up to 15 pounds (7 kilograms). The sea cow and the cormorant were hunted by humans for food.

HAWAII

More than 80 percent of Hawaii's original forest has been destroyed by fire, grazing, and agriculture. This has caused three hundred species of plants to vanish, while eighty are listed as **endangered**.

BIRDS

Today, forty of Hawaii's bird species are extinct. The Sandwich Island rail, *Porzana sandwichensis*, died out in 1884. It was killed off by introduced rats.

▲ These Hawaiian passerines were killed for their feathers and are now extinct.

Hawaiian passerines were killed for their feathers, which were used to make capes and headbands and to decorate helmets worn by tribal chiefs. The rare yellow feathers were particularly prized and were used to adorn the helmets of the great chiefs. Yellow feathers were provided by two species – *Drepanis pacifica,* a finch; and *Moho nobilis,* a honeyeater. Both species are extinct.

Hawaiian honeyeaters belonged to five species, only one of which still survives on Kauai. It is called o-o, and it is endangered. The Oahu o-o, *Moho apicalis,* became extinct in 1837. Bishop's o-o from Molokai, *Moho bishopi,* died out in 1904. The Great o-o of Hawaii, *Moho nobilis,* became extinct in 1934.

Less than a century ago, twenty-two species of finches from the Drepanididae family, native to Hawaii, survived.

Today, nine species have become extinct. The Oahu akepa, *Loxops coccinea rufa*, became extinct in 1893.

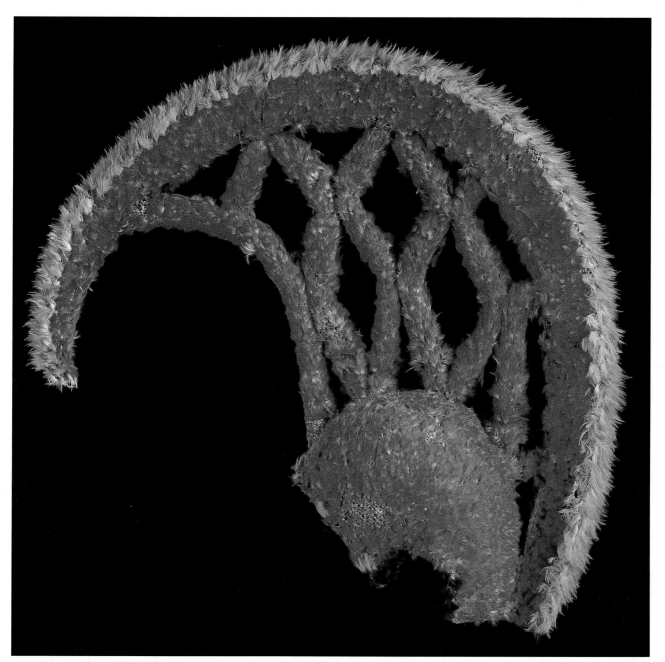

▲ This Hawaiian chief's helmet, or *mahiole*, is made of feathers from the passerine. The rare yellow feathers at the top of the helmet were particularly prized.

The Molokai Alauwahio, *Paroreomyza maculata flammea,* disappeared in 1937. The Koa finch, *Psittirostra palmeri,* lived on the slopes of the Mauna Lao volcano and disappeared by 1900. The Koa finch, *Loxioides flaviceps,* which lived on several of the islands, died out in 1981. The Kono finch, *Loxioides kona,* the smallest of the finches that lived on several of the Hawaiian islands, was last sighted in 1894. Many of these birds suffered from the introduction of cattle, predators, diseases, and **competitors**.

BONIN ISLANDS

The Bonin wood pigeon, *Columba versicolor,* was plentiful at the time of the islands' discovery, but the last known specimen was killed in 1889. Ten years earlier, the *Nycticorax caledonicus crassirostris,* a subspecies of the rufous night heron, became extinct.

WAKE

In the Pacific Ocean north of the Marshall Islands, Wake Island was the site of heavy fighting during World War II. When hungry Japanese troops were stationed on Wake, they ate the Wake Island rail, *Rallus wakensis,* into extinction.

▲ The Wake Island rail, *Rallus wakensis,* was exterminated by Japanese soldiers by 1944.

▲ The caracara, *Polyborus lutosus*, of the Mexican Island of Guadalupe, was last seen in 1900.

Caroline Islands

The Caroline Islands had a small rail, *Porzana monasa*, that disappeared by 1870. A starling from Kusaie Island, *Aplonis corvina*, became extinct about the same time. It was hunted by rats.

Iwo Jima

The island of Iwo Jima, south of Japan, was home to a native rail, *Poliolimnas cinereus brevipes*. This rail lived in the island's forests and was last sighted in 1924.

Guadalupe

The Mexican island of Guadalupe, located off the California coast and dominated by a mighty volcano, is today inhabited by tens of thousands of sheep and feral cats. Because of these predators, not even half of the island's original species survive today.

The Guadalupe Island storm petrel, *Oceanodroma macrodactyla*, was gone by 1911. The caracara, *Polyborus lutosus*, was a large, flightless bird of prey that ate **carrion**, rodents, insects, and worms. Farmers claimed it also killed their lambs, so this species was destroyed by 1900.

A subspecies of Bewick's wren, *Thyromanes bewickii brevicaudus*, was killed off by 1892 due to introduced cats.

NEW ZEALAND

New Zealand is made up of two of the largest islands in the South Pacific. The animals of these islands have taken heavy losses at the hands of humans.

FISH

The New Zealand grayling, *Prototroctes oxyrhynchus,* was an abundant food source for the native Maori people. This fish was extinct by 1923, due to the destruction of **habitat** by European settlers.

BIRDS

The black-footed parakeet, *Cyanoramphus novaezelandiae erythrotis,* made its home on Macquarie Island. The introduction of cats led to this bird's disappearance.

The New Zealand quail, *Coturnix novaezelandiae,* was plentiful at the beginning of the nineteenth century. Its numbers decreased rapidly due to overhunting, grassland fires, and introduction of predators. By 1875, the New Zealand quail had become extinct.

About thirteen species of giant birds, called moas, once lived in New Zealand. The moas grew to a little over 10 feet (3 meters) tall and could exceed 550 pounds (250 kg). They were hunted into extinction by 1875.

A laughing owl, *Sceloglaux albifacies,* inhabited New Zealand until it became extinct in 1914.

The merganser, *Mergus australis,* of the Auckland Islands, was extinct by 1905.

The huia, *Heteralocha acutirostris,* lived on the North Island of New Zealand. Its feathers were used in ceremonies and adorned the

▲ The moas of New Zealand could reach over 10 feet (3 m) in height.

cloaks of people who held high rank in the society. The last sighting of the huia was in 1907.

The Chatham Islands, east of mainland New Zealand, lost many animals to excessive hunting by humans and destruction of habitat caused by brush fires. The Chatham Island rail, *Cabalus modestus*, and Dieffenbach's rail, *Rallus philippensis dieffenbachi*, both became extinct in the nineteenth century.

NEW CALEDONIA

The first human settlements three thousand years ago on the island of New Caledonia destroyed most of its bigger animals. Cultivation of the coastal plains damaged the fauna and flora, causing the further extinction of species.

BIRDS

Sylviornis neocaledoniae was a giant galliforme. It probably

▲ The huia, *Heteralocha acutirostris*, was prized for its feathers that signified dignity and authority in early Maori lore.

disappeared before the arrival of the Europeans.

Extinct **diurnal** birds of prey include two species of goshawks, *Accipiter efficax* and *Accipiter quartus*, both of which disappeared before the arrival of Europeans to the island. These birds died out soon after their prey became extinct.

The rail, *Porphyrio kukwiedei*, a giant swamp hen, was hunted into extinction.

Two pigeons — a ground dove, *Gallicolumba longitarsus*, and a species similar to the Nicobar pigeon, *Caloenas canacorum* — are both extinct.

REPTILES

A type of crocodile, *Mekosuchus inexpectatus*, lived on giant birds, chickens, and other reptiles before its eventual extinction.

The tortoise, *Meiolania*, lived on the mainland of New Caledonia and on the islets of Tiga and Walpole in the Loyalty Islands. It was hunted into extinction by humans for food.

WALLIS ISLAND

Wallis Island was home to the Imperial pigeon, *Ducula david*, before its extinction due to hunting for sport.

LORD HOWE ISLAND

Lord Howe Island, east of Australia, was once inhabited by numerous bird species. The white-throated pigeon of the subspecies *Columba vitiensis godmanae* became extinct by 1853 due to hunting by humans.

▲ The extinct crocodile, *Mekosuchus inexpectatus*, had features that reminded scientists of the Mesozoic species.

A subspecies of the red-fronted parrot, *Cyanoramphus novaezelandiae subflavescens*, was exterminated by hunters by 1869 because humans thought the bird destroyed seeds and seedlings.

NORFOLK ISLAND

Norfolk Island is located halfway between New Zealand and New Caledonia. A native parrot, *Nestor*

▲ The parrot, *Nestor productus*, disappeared from Norfolk Island along with its habitat in 1851.

productus, became extinct by 1851 due to the destruction of its habitat. Humans hunted the Norfolk Island pigeon, *Hemiphaga novaezelandiae spadicea*, into extinction by 1801.

FIJI

The bar-winged rail, *Nesoclopeus poeciloptera*, inhabited marshy areas and was unable to fly. It became extinct as a result of habitat destruction and

▲ A giant swamp hen, *Porphyrio albus*, lived on Lord Howe Island.

hunting by introduced rats and mongooses.

SOLOMON ISLANDS AND VANUATU

Meek's pigeon, *Microgoura meeki*, of Choiseul in the Solomon Islands, was seen for the first and last time in 1904. It was hunted by humans and cats.

A dove, *Gallicolumba ferruginea*, lived on Tanna, one of the islands of Vanuatu. It was extinct by 1774.

GALÁPAGOS ISLANDS

The Galápagos Islands, located in the Pacific Ocean east of Ecuador, is one of the world's most famous nature **reserves**. The unique fauna, closely studied by the naturalist Charles Darwin, includes a diverse group of at least fourteen subspecies of the tortoise, *Geochelone elephantopus*, each native to a particular island of the group.

▲ The Meek's pigeon, *Microgoura meeki*, now extinct, lived in the Solomon Islands.

Within three hundred years, four of these subspecies have become extinct.

TAHITI

Tahiti was once home to a sandpiper, *Prosobonia leucoptera*. The bird's habitat was invaded by introduced pigs, dogs, and cats that destroyed the young in their nests. The Tahitian black-fronted parrot, *Cyanoramphus zealandicus*, disappeared in the 1850s.

THREE THOUSAND ISLANDS

The Indian Ocean contains more than three thousand islands in its 12 million square miles (31 million sq. km) of water surface.

The actions of humans have caused approximately sixty species of animals on these islands to become extinct. The uncertain future for the remaining species that inhabit Indian Ocean islands is cause for deep concern.

▲ Birds are often the victims of hunting by humans. The *Alectroenas nitidissima* of Mauritius became extinct by 1826.

THE MASCARENES

European settlers first visited the Mascarene Islands – Mauritius, Réunion, and Rodrigues – in 1500. Hunting and the introduction of rats, cats, dogs, pigs, and other livestock brought about the rapid extinction of nearly thirty species of birds and seven species of reptiles.

BIRDS

The number of bird species extinct at the hands of humans on the Mascarenes stands at seven species of parrots, three species of pigeons, two species of ducks, two species of herons, four species of rails, one grebe species, one darter species, six species of birds of prey, and one eagle species. The extinction of most of these species took place during the eighteenth century.

The dodo bird has become a symbol of extinction. Dodoes

▲ The white dodo of Réunion, *Raphus solitarius*, was solitary in its habits. It was extinct by 1746.

were about 30 inches (75 cm) long and flightless. They were gray, white, or yellow. Three species of dodoes were extinct on Mauritius in 1681, on Réunion in 1746, and on Rodrigues by 1790. The dodo was hunted into extinction by humans.

Although most extinctions in the Mascarenes occurred in the eighteenth century, the last known Daubenton's starling, *Fregilupus varius*, was sighted in 1840. The last known Mascarene parrot, *Mascarinus mascarinus*, lived in captivity until 1834.

23

REPTILES

Extinct Mascarene reptiles include a small lizard, *Leiolopisma mauritiana*, two species of diurnal geckos, *Phelsuma*, and five land tortoises, *Cylindraspis*.

MADAGASCAR

Madagascar lies off the eastern coast of southern Africa. By the time the first European settlers arrived there in the sixteenth century, twenty species of **vertebrates** were already extinct. The species that have survived are endangered. The extinctions were mainly caused by hunting, but brush fires destroyed a major part of the forest cover that sheltered many large animal species.

BIRDS

At one time, there was a large collection of flightless birds on Madagascar. The largest species, *Aepyornis maximus*, was over 10 feet (3 m) tall.

These giant birds became extinct in the seventeenth century due to hunting.

REPTILES

Two giant tortoise species from Madagascar are extinct. The shell of *Dipsochelis (Geochelone) grandidieri*, the largest species, was more than 4.5 feet (1.4 m) long.

▲ *Aepyornis maximus* was one of the largest land birds ever known.

▲ This lemur, *Megaladapis*, is thought to have survived until the seventeenth century. It was 6.5 feet (2 m) long.

MAMMALS

Among Madagascar's extinct mammals are two small hippopotamus species. They were only about 7 feet (2.1 m) long and 3 feet (1 m) high and may have survived until the twentieth century.

At least three species of rodents have died out on Madagascar. But primates called lemurs have suffered the greatest losses. Forest fires caused the land to dry up and brought about a vast decrease in the forest cover, greatly reducing the habitat of these animals. The last of the lemurs may have been killed by dogs during the seventeenth century.

MEDITERRANEAN SEA

AN EVOLUTION

Most native species to the Mediterranean islands were destroyed at the hands of humans. As with all island environments, the biggest and most desirable species disappeared first as a result of hunting. The main islands — Corsica and Sardinia, Sicily, the Balearics, Crete, Cyprus, and the Cyclades — then witnessed the evolution of new fauna introduced from Europe and Africa. The islands thereafter became home to new types of elephants, hippopotamuses, and deer — in dwarf form.

BIRDS

The Cretan owl, *Athene cretensis*, was a nocturnal bird of prey. It is known only from fossils and may have been 2 feet (60 cm) tall.

MAMMALS

Perhaps the most unusual extinct species that once inhabited the Mediterranean islands was the pygmy elephant, *Elephas falconeri.* It was related to African

▲ The Cretan owl, *Athene cretensis,* was able to fly only short distances and spent most of its time walking on the ground.

▲ The remarkable pygmy elephant of Sicily, *Elephas falconeri,* is now extinct.

elephants, but it was only 3-5 feet (90-152 cm) tall.

A pygmy subspecies of deer native to the island of Corsica, *Cervus elaphus corsicanus*, is probably extinct today. Deer of the *Candiacervus* genus on the island of Crete had club-shaped antlers and are known only from fossils. These tiny deer became extinct due to overhunting by humans and cultivation of the land.

▲ The smallest of the pygmy deer of the genus *Candiacervus* stood only 16 inches (40 cm) high.

▲ The Mediterranean rodent, *Prolagus corsicanus*, similar to a cross between a rabbit and a guinea pig, was hunted by humans into extinction.

These are but a few examples of wildlife species that are lost forever. In order to avoid the human errors of the past that have led to the senseless destruction of wildlife, each of us must take responsibility and get involved to protect endangered animals and their habitats.

SCIENTIFIC NAMES OF ANIMALS IN THIS BOOK

Animals have different names in every language. To simplify matters, researchers the world over have agreed to use the same scientific names, usually from ancient Greek or Latin, to identify animals. With this in mind, most animals are classified by two names. One is the genus name; the other is the name of the species to which they belong. Additional names indicate further subgroupings. The scientific names for most of the animals included in *Lost Forever: Extinct Animals of the Islands* are:

Bar-winged rail . . . . *Nesoclopeus poeciloptera*
Bering Island spectacled cormorant . . . .
. . . . *Phalacrocorax perspicillatus*
Bewick's wren
. . . . *Thyromanes bewickii brevicaudus*
Bishop's o-o . . . . *Moho bishopi*
Black-footed parakeet . . . .
. . . . *Cyanoramphus novaezelandiae erythrotis*
Black-fronted parrot . *Cyanoramphus zealandicus*
Bonin wood pigeon . . . . *Columba versicolor*
Cape Verde giant skink . . . . *Macroscincus coctaei*
Caribbean monk seal . . . . . *Monachus tropicalis*
Caroline Islands rail . . . . *Porzana monasa*
Chatham Island rail . . . . *Cabalus modestus*
Cretan owl . . . . *Athene cretensis*
Cuban ground sloth . . . . *Megalocnus*
Cuban macaw . . . . *Ara tricolor*
Daubenton's starling . . . . *Fregilupus varius*
Dieffenbach's rail . *Rallus philippensis dieffenbachi*
Falklands fox . . . . *Dusicyon australis*
Giant galliforme . . . . . *Sylviornis neocaledoniae*
Great auk . . . . *Pinguinis impennis*
Guadalupe Island storm petrel . . . .
. . . . *Oceanodroma macrodactyla*
Huia . . . . *Heteralocha acutirostris*
Imperial pigeon . . . . *Ducula david*
Isolobodons (2 species) . . . . . . *Isolobodon levir*
. . . . *Isolobodon portoricensis*
Iwo Jima rail . . . . . . *Poliolimnas cinereus brevipes*
Jamaican nightjar . . . . . *Siphonornis americanus*
Kono finch . . . . *Loxioides kona*
Kusaie Island starling . . . . *Aplonis corvina*

Laughing owl . . . . *Sceloglaux albifacies*
Mascarene parrot . . . . . *Mascarinus mascarinus*
Meek's pigeon . . . . *Microgoura meeki*
Molokai Alauwahio . . . .
. . . . *Paroreomyza maculata flammea*
New Zealand grayling . . *Prototroctes oxyrhynchus*
New Zealand quail . . . . *Coturnix novaezelandiae*
Norfolk Island parrot . . . . *Nestor productus*
Oahu akepa . . . . *Loxops coccinea rufa*
Oahu o-o . . . . *Moho apicalis*
Orange-bellied macaw
. . . . *Anodorhynchus martinicus*
Passerines (2 species) . . . . *Drepanis pacifica*
. . . . *Moho nobilis*
Pygmy deer . . . . *Cervus elaphus corsicanus*
Pygmy elephant . . . . *Elephas falconeri*
Red-fronted parrot . . . .
. . *Cyanoramphus novaezelandiae subflavescens*
Rufous night heron . . . .
. . . . *Nycticorax caledonicus crassirostris*
Sandwich Island rail . . . . *Porzana sandwichensis*
Steller's sea cow . . . . *Hydrodamalis stelleri*
Tahitian sandpiper . . . . . . *Prosobonia leucoptera*
Tanna dove . . . . *Gallicolumba ferruginea*
Tristan gallinule . . . . *Gallinula nesiotis*
Violet macaw . . . . . *Anodorhynchus purpurescens*
Wake Island rail . . . . *Rallus wakensis*
White dodo . . . . *Raphus solitarius*
White-throated pigeon . . . .
. . . . *Columba vitiensis godmanae*
Yellow-headed macaw . . . . *Ara gossei*

GLOSSARY

archipelago — a group of islands.

carrion — dead and rotting animal flesh.

competitors — animal species that must struggle with other animal species to obtain food and habitat.

diurnal — active during daylight hours.

edentate — having no teeth.

endangered — in peril of dying out, or becoming extinct.

extinction — the condition of no longer surviving on Earth.

fauna — a region's animal life.

habitat — an environment where plants and animals live and grow.

introduced predators — animals brought by humans into a new environment where they kill the native animals and plants for food.

reserves — areas of land set aside for the protection of animals and plants.

species — a grouping of animals that share similar characteristics.

vertebrates — animal species that have a backbone.

MORE BOOKS TO READ

Animal Extinctions: What Everyone Should Know. R. J. Hoage, ed. (Smithsonian)

The Doomsday Book of Animals: A Natural History of Vanished Species. (Penguin)

Endangered! (series). Bob Burton (Gareth Stevens)

Environment Alert! Vanishing Rain Forests. Paula Hogan (Gareth Stevens)

The Extinct Species Collection (series). (Gareth Stevens)

In Peril! (series). Barbara J. Behm and J-C Balouet (Gareth Stevens)

VIDEOS

The Dragons of Galápagos. (The Undersea World of Jacques Cousteau)

The Humpbacks of Maui. (Pacific Whale Foundation)

Realm of the Alligator. (National Geographic)

The Unsinkable Sea Otter. (The Undersea World of Jacques Cousteau)

WEB SITES

http://envirolink.org/

http://netvet.wustl.edu/wildlife.htm

PLACES TO WRITE

The following organizations educate people about animals, promote the protection of animals, and encourage the conservation of natural habitat. Include a self-addressed, stamped envelope for a reply.

The Cousteau Society, Inc.
870 Greenbriar Circle
Suite 402
Chesapeake, VA 23320

Canadian Wildlife
   Federation
2740 Queensview Drive
Ottawa, Ontario K2B 1A2

World Wildlife Fund
1250 24th Street, N.W.
Washington, D.C. 20037

Greenpeace
1436 U Street, N.W.
Washington, D.C. 20009

Canadian Nature
   Federation
One Nicholas Street
Suite 520
Ottawa, Ontario K1N 7B7

Royal Society for the
   Prevention of Cruelty
   to Animals
3 Burwood Highway
Burwood East
Victoria 3151 Australia

International Fund for
   Animal Welfare
P.O. Box 2587
Rivonia 2128, South Africa

International Fund for
   Animal Welfare
P.O. Box 56
Paddington, New South
   Wales 2021
Australia

Department of
   Conservation
P.O. Box 10-420
Wellington, New Zealand

Sea Shepherd Conservation
   Society
P.O. Box 628
Venice, CA 90294

ACTIVITIES TO HELP SAVE ENDANGERED SPECIES

1. Write the United States Department of the Interior, Publications Unit, Fish and Wildlife Service, Washington, D.C., 20240, for a list of endangered wildlife. Then write to government officials and express your support for the protection of these animals and their habitat. Also, write to government officials to express your support for strengthening the Endangered Species Act.

2. Contact a nature organization in your area. Ask how you can become involved in saving wildlife.

3. Do not buy wild or exotic animals as pets. Also, do not buy fur, bearskin rugs, ivory, or any other products that endanger animals.

4. Visit an exhibit at a natural history museum where there are replicas of extinct animals. Or spend a day at the zoo. Are any of the animals you see endangered?

INDEX